NIGHT SKY NAVIGATOR

OBSERVER'S GUIDE TO THE STARS, CONSTELLATIONS, AND PLANETS

KENNETH HEWITT-WHITE

ILLUSTRATIONS BY KATHRYN ADAMS
HOLOGRAMS BY MICHAEL PAGE
DIAGRAMS BY ENRICO VARRASSO

SOMERVILLE HOUSE, USA

ISBN 1-58184-067-5
A B C D E F G H I J

Printed in Canada

Art Direction & Design:
David Thorne Communications

Somerville House, USA is distributed by
Penguin Putnam Books for Young Readers,
345 Hudson Street, NY 10014

Published in Canada by
Somerville House Publishing
a division of Somerville House Books Limited
3080 Yonge Street, Suite 5000
Toronto, ON M4N 3N1

e-mail: sombooks@goodmedia.com
website: www.sombooks.com

*To my constant partner, Lynda, who supported this idea from the
beginning, and to my niece, Whitney, who represents the little
stargazer in all of us.* — K.H.W.

Author's acknowledgements
My thanks to Terence Dickinson for his early input into the
project and for his invaluable review of the manuscript. I am
indebted to Margaret McClintock for her patient analysis of
every element in *The Holographic Night Sky* package.

Hologram Team: Michael Page with William Cameron,
William Chang, Alex Laverick, Khalid Mokhtarzada, and
Thomas J. Cvetkovich. Thanks to the Photon League and
the Ontario College of Art and Design.

"How the Holograms Were Made" illustration on back cover
by William Chang

CONTENTS

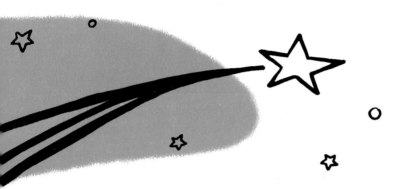

INTRODUCTION

Humans have always been fascinated by the night sky. Today our view of the night sky is often dimmed by the lights of cities, but long ago, people stood in awe of a celestial panorama filled with thousands of stars. The pinpoints of starlight seemed to shine down from heaven itself.

The astronomer-priests of ancient times did not have enough knowledge of science to understand the cosmos. They believed there was a connection between the stars and planets overhead and events on Earth. Generations of sky watchers memorized the patterns made by groups of stars in the sky. In these patterns, or *constellations*, they saw portraits of mythical heroes and strange creatures. People's fears and hopes, their struggles against the forces of nature, and their dreams for a better life were all symbolized in the vivid characters of the starry heavens.

Stargazing had a practical side, too. Knowing the positions of the constellations and how they moved throughout the night and year gave sailors their directions and enabled them to navigate the open sea. By following the cycles of the Sun and Moon, astronomers could keep track of time and accurately define the seasons. For farmers, the changing night sky was a calendar signaling the times for planting and harvesting crops. Stargazing was central to the development of ancient civilizations. The stars were familiar to people everywhere.

Go outside at night and look up. The starry pageant overhead is your link to the imaginations of the earliest peoples on Earth. The *Holographic Night Sky* kit is your key to their universe — the constellations they created and the mysterious motions of the Moon and planets they marveled at.

BE A NIGHT SKY NAVIGATOR

Explore the constellations from your own back yard. Everything you need to become an expert night sky navigator is included in the *Holographic Night Sky* kit. The *Night Sky Navigator* will guide the way. In this book, you will learn about constellations, stars, and planets and how to find them. No telescope is needed. All the stars listed here can be spotted with the naked eye.

In the eight Constellation Holograms, made to be placed in this book, the ancient myths and characters of the starry night sky spring to life.

Take your Star Charts with you whenever you head outdoors to identify stars. They include a star chart for each season to help you to locate all the constellations described in this book.

It takes only a few seconds for your eyes to adjust to a bright lamp indoors, but it takes several minutes for your pupils to open up enough to let in the much fainter starlight outside. With the red-filter Observer's Light, you can read the Star Charts without affecting your night vision.

Take your *Observer's Handbook* on your stargazing expeditions, too. It explains how to use the Star Charts, describes how to observe the best sky targets in more detail using binoculars, and includes activities that show you fun ways of understanding the night sky.

As you locate constellations, planets, and stars, check them off in the logs at the back of the handbook. Soon you will have an impressive list of sightings to show your family and friends.

THE HOLOGRAMS

T he Constellation Holograms will help you to visualize sky characters such as **Aquarius**, the Water Carrier. To view the holograms, hold them under direct sunlight, or under a spotlight or directional light source. Then, tilt them from side to side.

The best season to look for each constellation in the sky is indicated by the landscape in the hologram. When you go stargazing, bear in mind that the eight different constellations in the holograms are not in proportion to one another. A constellation's stars may not be as bright as they seem in the hologram. You will also notice that, depending on the time of night and the season (and where you live), a constellation may appear low or high in the sky, upright or at an angle — or even upside down! In this book, you'll find out why.

HOW THE HOLOGRAMS WERE MADE

F irst, a 3-D representation of the constellation character was constructed in a computer, using 3-D animation software. Then, a virtual camera was moved around the character to create a series of 2-D images showing it from different angles. A separate computer fed these images to a holographic printer, a computer-controlled robotic device.

A holographic printer uses the light from a laser beam to record images onto holographic film. The laser beam is split in two by a beam splitter. The two beams are then spread by lenses called beam expanders. The object beam illuminates a liquid crystal display (LCD) that is backed by a diffusion panel. The LCD presents the 2-D images to be recorded on the holographic film. The reference beam illuminates the film from a 45° angle. (Nothing can move more than a few billionths of an inch; therefore, a vibration isolation system is used to keep everything still.)

The two laser beams interact to form a thin vertical strip on the film. Using a translating slit, the printer creates a series of strips, one for each of the 2-D images recorded by the virtual camera.

When you look at a hologram, each eye sees the constellation character from a slightly different viewpoint. Your brain interprets this as a 3-D scene.

"How the Holograms Were Made" is illustrated on the back cover of this book.

AQUARIUS, THE WATER CARRIER

Aquarius is not an easy star pattern to see, but it was considered important in ancient times. The Sun passed through Aquarius every spring, just as the rainy season began, and for many ancient peoples, this constellation was connected with water. The Egyptians imagined the Water Carrier emptying his bucket into the Nile River, thus initiating the spring rains and annual floods that kept the Nile Delta green. On the other hand, the ancient Babylonians saw the passage of the Sun through Aquarius as a bad omen. They didn't like the rainy season! In fact, they blamed Aquarius for the flood described in their biblical epic, Gilgamesh.

 Best time to look: September through December. See Autumn Star Chart.

YOU ARE
HERE

IT'S YOUR UNIVERSE!

A TINY EARTH...

Earth is small and isolated. The closest celestial body to our planet is the Moon. It would take nearly six months to travel between Earth and the Moon if you could go only as fast as a car. It's a good thing we have rockets. Still, it takes a spacecraft several days to reach the Moon.

Our *solar system* includes our own star, the Sun, the nine planets that revolve around it, at least 60 moons, thousands of rocky worlds called *asteroids*, and uncountable dirty snowballs of frozen gas and dust called *comets*. A space mission to Pluto, the most distant planet in our solar system, would take more than 10 years by rocket — one way.

A BIG MILKY WAY…

We are residents of a vast city of stars, or *galaxy*, called the Milky Way. Viewed from outside and far away, the Milky Way would look like a hazy, spiral cloud. The Milky Way galaxy is so big that light itself — traveling millions of times faster than a car — takes roughly 90,000 *years* to cross it. We therefore say that the Milky Way is 90,000 light-years wide. Our galaxy is truly immense.

When you stare into space from your back yard, almost everything you see belongs to just a small portion of the Milky Way galaxy.

AND LOTS AND LOTS OF GALAXIES

The Milky Way is only one of countless millions of galaxies in the universe. At mountaintop observatories, astronomers — scientists who study objects in the cosmos — use large telescopes to peer beyond our Milky Way to other galaxies unimaginably far away. Galaxies come in various shapes and sizes. Like snowflakes, no two are alike.

Amazingly, all the galaxies are rushing away from each other. Space itself is stretching, carrying the galaxies outwards. In other words, the universe is expanding. Most scientists think the universe began 12 to 15 billion years ago in an explosive event called the Big Bang (though what caused the Big Bang, and whether anything existed before it, is not known). Stars, planets, and galaxies have been forming ever since.

Our family of planets whirls around the Sun. The enormous Milky Way wheels in space, carrying our solar system with it. Distant galaxies race apart at high speed due to the force of the Big Bang. Observing the night sky is not only fun, it makes you feel part of all this action. It's *your* universe.

THE LOWDOWN ON LIGHT-YEARS

With a speed of about 186,000 miles per second (300,000 km/sec), light is the fastest thing we know of. A beam of light travels about 6 *trillion* miles (9 trillion km) in one year. We call that unit of measure a *light-year*. The distances to objects in the cosmos are measured in light-years because using miles or kilometers would involve hopelessly large numbers. In a way, light-years take us back in time. If a star is 70 light-years away, it means that the light we see from that star tonight left the star 70 years ago.

THE SKY SPHERE

When we gaze up at the night sky, we see stars in every direction. We can't tell that the stars are scattered over vast distances in space. They all look the same distance away. Just for fun, imagine that all the stars are stuck to an invisible sphere surrounding our planet. We call this illusion the *sky sphere*.

Now imagine an invisible line connecting Earth's North and South Poles. We call this imaginary line Earth's *axis*. Earth spins once around on its axis every 24 hours, creating another amazing illusion. The turning Earth makes the sky sphere seem to turn in the *opposite* direction.

The rotating sky sphere carries all the celestial objects with it, making them rise and set. In the day, we see a bowl of blue with the Sun in it. At night, the bowl fades to black and fills up with the Moon, planets, and stars. No matter where and when we look, we see half of the slowly turning sky sphere at all times.

WHAT IS A STAR?

Substances can exist as a solid, a liquid, or a *gas*. The simplest and most plentiful substance in the universe is the gas called *hydrogen*. For most of its life, a *star* is a huge ball of hydrogen gas. A star's hydrogen burns so fiercely that stars are far hotter than anything on Earth. Their temperatures range from thousands of degrees on the surface to millions of degrees inside. This heat creates light and makes the stars shine. Stars don't burn forever, but some can last billions of years.

Our Sun, with a diameter of 870,000 miles (1.4 million km), is a star of average size and temperature. It is a middle-aged star, about 5 billion years old.

The stars are spread out through immense distances in space. The Sun is about 93 million miles (150 million km) away from Earth. The nearest star to our sun is actually a trio, called the Alpha Centauri group. The Alpha Centauri family is a little over four light-years away. The most distant stars you can see with your naked eyes are several thousand light-years away, near the edge of our Milky Way.

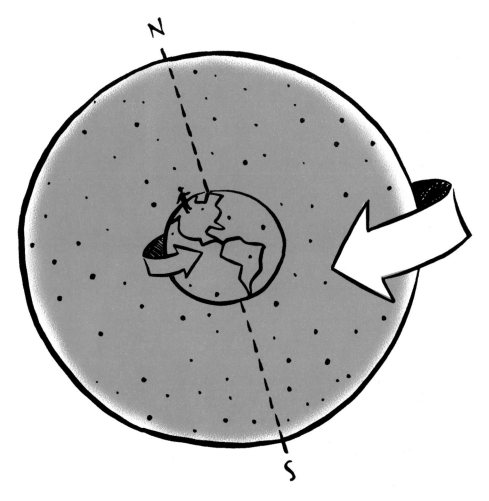

No matter where you are on Earth, at night you see a bowl of stars wheeling overhead. The stars remain fixed but Earth rotates, making the sky sphere seem to move in the opposite direction. The portion of the sky sphere you see depends on the time of night, the season, and how far north or south you live.

★ LOOK IN THE HANDBOOK

How can a telephone pole show you that Earth is moving? See "Catch the Drift" on page 7 of the *Observer's Handbook*.

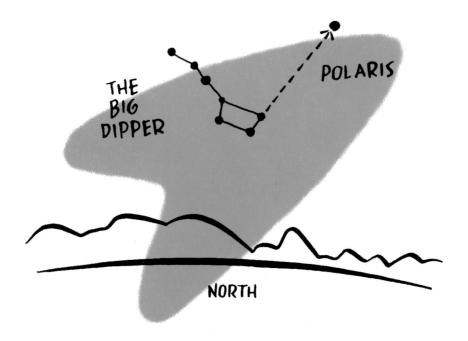

THE BIG DIPPER

POLARIS

NORTH

KNOW YOUR NEWS

NEWS stands for North, East, West, and South — the four main directions. Knowing your directions will help you find sky objects more quickly. You can easily learn to find your directions, day or night, without a compass.

Look at the illustration on page 11 again. You'll see that, like Earth, the sky has a north and south pole. The sky pole we see from North America is called the North Celestial Pole. The star closest to the North Celestial Pole is called Polaris. This bright star, residing 430 light-years away, is also known as the North Star.

KNOWING THEIR

NAMES

Polaris *(poh-LAIR-iss)*

To locate the North Star, first look for the seven bright stars of the **Big Dipper**. With its distinctive handle and bowl, the Big Dipper is easy to identify. At the end of the Dipper's bowl, two stars called the *pointers* aim at Polaris every night. When you face Polaris, you face north. Behind you is south. East is on your right, and west is on your left. Now you know your *NEWS*.

Knowing your directions is a big help at night. If you face east, you will see the stars rising. Face west to see where the stars set. Most of the stars in the north don't rise or set as they turn. You can see them all night. You'll find out why on the next page.

You can find your *NEWS* in the daytime as well. Where the Sun rises is roughly east, and where it sets is roughly west. At its highest point in between (which occurs about noon), the Sun is due south. Opposite that point is north.

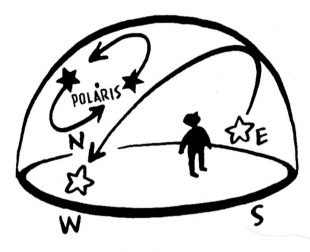

Stars rise in the eastern half of the sky, track across the south, then set in the west. But in the north, the stars go around in complete circles without rising or setting.

STAR MAGNITUDES

We use the term *magnitude* to describe a star's brightness. The smaller the magnitude number, the brighter the star. For example, magnitude 1 is very bright. Stars of magnitude 5 are dim. On the charts in this book, bigger dots mean brighter stars.

Compare the dots in the illustration on page 12. Polaris, magnitude 2, is about as bright as the stars in the Big Dipper, but it is a lot farther away.

How bright a star appears to us depends mostly on its distance from us and its size. A large star that is far away can appear much brighter than a nearby small star.

MOTION BY THE HOUR

O n the next clear night, check the stars every hour or so. You will see that they have moved from when you last looked. Because Earth spins on its axis, the sky show is constantly in motion. The line where the sky and Earth meet is called the *horizon*. As Earth turns on its axis, different stars and constellations appear above the horizon and disappear below it.

Turn your back to Polaris and face south. Then east is on your left, and west is on your right. The stars seem to rise in the east and set in the west.

With experience, you will notice that not many stars rise and set exactly in the east and west. Some stars rise in the southeast and set in the southwest. They swing in low arcs over the south horizon, peeking between buildings and trees as they go. More northerly stars rise in the northeast and arc high overhead before setting in the northwest.

If you could stay outside all night long and check the stars near Polaris, you would find that they never go below the horizon. These stars, which circle the North Celestial Pole without rising or setting, are called *circumpolar stars*. The *circumpolar constellations* are constellations that circle the pole. We'll get to know them better on pages 20–23.

WHY DO STARS TWINKLE?

V iewed from outer space, stars do not twinkle. From Earth, however, we look at the stars through an ocean of air. Earth's *atmosphere* — the layer of air that surrounds Earth — is always in motion, and this *turbulence* makes the stars appear to twinkle.

Stars are huge, but they are so far away that, even through the biggest telescopes, we see them only as points of light.

The tiny threads of starlight entering our atmosphere are easily rippled by turbulence.

When you look at stars near the horizon, you are looking through more air than when you look overhead, so the stars twinkle even more. Different temperatures in different layers of the atmosphere create a prism effect, making these stars actually change color as they twinkle.

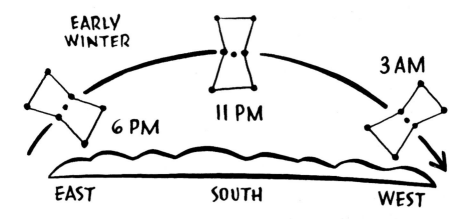

Face south. Here, we see the constellation Orion rising in the east, cresting in the south, then setting in the west.

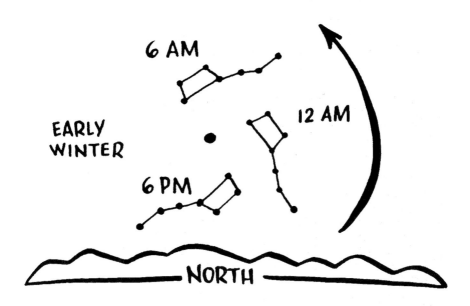

Face north. While most stars appear to travel across the sky during the night, those in the north turn in tight circles around the North Celestial Pole. This spot is marked by Polaris, which acts like the hub of a wheel. The Big Dipper circles around Polaris once every 24 hours. If you live in the northern United States or Canada, the Big Dipper never sets.

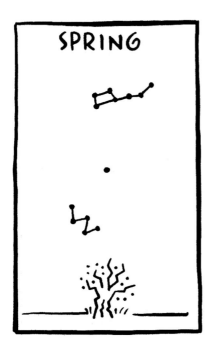

MOTION THROUGH THE YEAR

Gravity is a force that pulls objects toward each other. Bigger objects pull smaller objects toward them, and the closer they are, the more they pull. Compared to the planets, the Sun is huge. The Sun's gravity causes the planets to *orbit*, or go around, the Sun, rather than drift off to another part of the galaxy.

Traveling through space at more than 60,000 miles per hour (100 000 kph) — a thousand times faster than a car — Earth completes its long orbit around the Sun once a year. As Earth travels, it gradually gives us views of different groups of constellations. Each night, the constellations descend in the west a few minutes earlier than the night before. After a couple of weeks, they set almost an hour earlier. Eventually, they disappear for the season. New star patterns arriving in the east

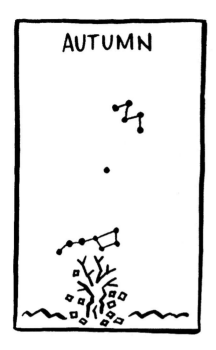

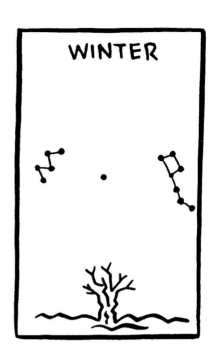

Here, we see two of the circumpolar constellations, the Big Dipper and Cassiopeia, circling slowly around Polaris as the seasons progress.

replace the departing constellations, which will return a year later.

As the year goes by, the circumpolar constellations appear to rotate slowly around the North Celestial Pole.

THE SOUTHERN SKY

In North America, we see many different stars throughout the year, but the south horizon always hides part of the view. People who live farther south, in South America, Africa, southern Asia, and Australia, see the constellations that are hidden from us. The most famous of these is the **Southern Cross**, which early explorers used as a guide during their long ocean voyages in the Southern Hemisphere. If a dedicated stargazer were to visit a country near Earth's equator and watch the sky for a year, he or she could see every one of the constellations in the northern and southern skies.

CASSIOPEIA ORION

LEO THE TEAPOT

You'll need your imagination to visualize the objects and characters in the night sky. The holograms and sky myths in this book will help you to see how pictures can be formed from random groups of stars. This illustration shows both ancient characters and a modern sky figure, the Teapot — another name for Sagittarius.

INTRODUCING THE CONSTELLATIONS

Welcome to a colorful cast of celestial characters. Scattered among the stars are kings and queens, heroes and villains, and wild creatures of every description. You can see them all in the magnificent pageant of constellations that parades across the sky every clear night.

Thousands of years ago, people looked up at the stars and imagined patterns among them. The ancients brought the night sky to life with their constellation pictures. They made up elaborate stories, or *myths*, in which these strange sky characters played prominent roles. Star stories were told all over the world. Every culture created its own myths.

Some of the constellations do look like stick figures of animals or people. Good examples are Leo, the Lion, and Orion, the Hunter. But most constellation patterns we recognize today don't resemble their mythological namesakes at all. Instead, the modern sky is full of houses, teapots, kites, crosses, triangles, squares, and rectangles — even letters of the alphabet.

ABOUT STAR AND CONSTELLATION NAMES

There is no actual connection among the stars in a constellation. Although they appear to be in the same part of the sky, the stars of a constellation are usually separated by huge distances. We merely imagine the connect-the-dots pattern of a constellation.

Most of the constellations we know were named by the Greeks and Babylonians between 2,500 and 5,000 years ago, to help with time-keeping and navigation and also to satisfy religious beliefs.

Many of the constellations represent characters from Greek mythology, but most of their individual stars have Arabic names. Astronomers of the Middle East translated the names given to the stars by the Greeks hundreds of years before.

FRIENDS OF THE NORTH STAR

T he stars in the northern sky are like constant friends because you can find them any time. Let's take a closer look at these circumpolar constellations. Polaris, the North Star, is the brightest star in the **Little Dipper**. It's the star at the end of the Little Dipper's handle. Two other stars nearly as bright are located at the end of the Little Dipper's bowl. They are nicknamed the Guardians of the Pole, because they march around the North Celestial Pole in such a small circle.

The Big and Little Dippers are portions of **Ursa Major**, which means "Great Bear," and **Ursa Minor**, which means "Little Bear." The two bears have long tails you won't see on real bears. The bear shapes are difficult to trace among the many faint stars in the north sky.

Opposite the Big Dipper from Polaris is Queen **Cassiopeia**, sometimes known as the Lady in the Chair. Her brightest stars form a W in spring, when she is low in the sky, and an M in fall, when she appears high overhead. Either way, Cassiopeia is easy to identify.

At the queen's side is fainter **Cepheus**, the King of Ethiopia. Cepheus contains five stars of average brightness that form the shape of a house with a steep roof. Sliding between the two Dippers is **Draco**, the Dragon. Four stars give Draco a distinctive head, but it takes practice to pick out the stars marking his long, curving body.

KNOWING THEIR NAMES

Alcor (AL-core)
Cassiopeia (KAS-ee-oh-PEE-ah)
Cepheus (SEE-fee-us)
Draco (DRAY-ko)
Mizar (MY-zar)
Ursa Major (ER-sah MAY-jer)
Ursa Minor (ER-sah MY-ner)

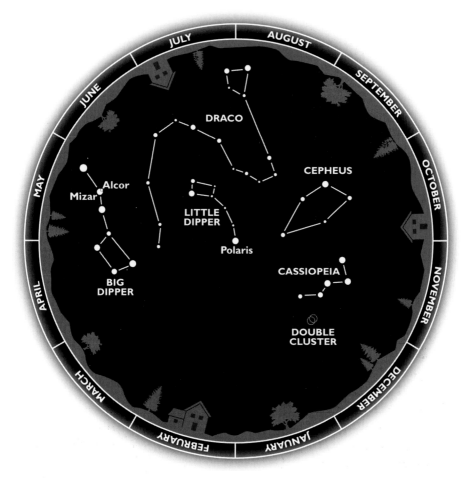

Face north. Turn the page so the current month appears at the top. The positions of the stars in the sky will roughly match those on the chart.

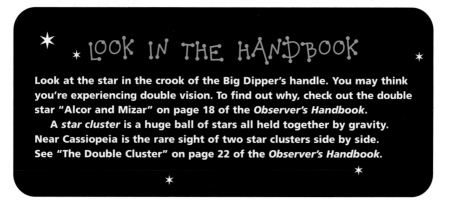

✶ ✶ LOOK IN THE HANDBOOK ✶

Look at the star in the crook of the Big Dipper's handle. You may think you're experiencing double vision. To find out why, check out the double star "Alcor and Mizar" on page 18 of the *Observer's Handbook*.

A *star cluster* is a huge ball of stars all held together by gravity. Near Cassiopeia is the rare sight of two star clusters side by side. See "The Double Cluster" on page 22 of the *Observer's Handbook*.

URSA MAJOR, THE GREAT BEAR

According to Greek legend, Zeus, the king of the gods, gave Ursa Major and Ursa Minor immortality when he grabbed them by their stubby tails and flung them into the starry heavens, stretching their tails in the process.

In Native American sky lore, the annual movement of the Big Dipper around Polaris symbolized a bear hunt. Bears emerged from hibernation every spring as the constellation rose overhead. The Dipper's bowl represented Spirit Bear, and the stars in the Dipper's handle were three hunters in hot pursuit. They would chase Spirit Bear all summer until he weakened and drifted nearer to the horizon. In the fall, Spirit Bear reached his lowest point and the hunters attacked and killed him. Fortunately, the soul of Spirit Bear is immortal. After a long winter's sleep, another bear appears and the cycle begins again. Variations on this story appear in the traditions of several Native American peoples, including the Micmac, the Iroquois, and the Cherokee nations.

 Best time to look: Any clear night. See any Star Chart.

CASSIOPEIA, THE QUEEN OF ETHIOPIA

In Greek mythology, Queen Cassiopeia boasted that she was more beautiful than anyone. As punishment for her vanity, the gods removed her from her palace in Ethiopia and placed her in the northern sky. There her throne hangs upside down — with poor Cassiopeia holding on for dear life — every winter and spring.

Some Arab astonomers pictured this W of stars as a hand. Others saw the hump of a camel. The Laplanders of northern Europe imagined an elk's antlers. Canada's Inuit, to whom Cassiopeia is constantly visible during the dark Arctic winter, see its three brightest stars as a triangular stand for a seal-oil lamp. Natives of the Marshall Islands watch the W dip into the Pacific Ocean each night like the tail fin of a heavenly porpoise.

 Best time to look: Any clear night. See any Star Chart.

THE LION IN SPRING

Without a doubt, springtime's best constellation is **Leo**, the Lion. The lion stick-figure is easy to pick out. Look for the lion's face in the six stars that look like a backwards question mark. The dot at the bottom of the question mark is Leo's brightest star, Regulus, 78 light-years from Earth and the heart of the celestial lion. Leo's hindquarters are marked by a big triangle of stars.

Leo is a member of the *zodiac*, the band of constellations through which the planets drift. (The zodiac is explained in more detail on pages 44–45.) Beware. The shape of the lion is occasionally distorted by a traveling planet masquerading as a bright star.

KNOWING THEIR
NAMES

Denebola
(duh-NEB-oh-lah)
Leo *(LEE-oh)*
Regulus *(REGG-u-lus)*

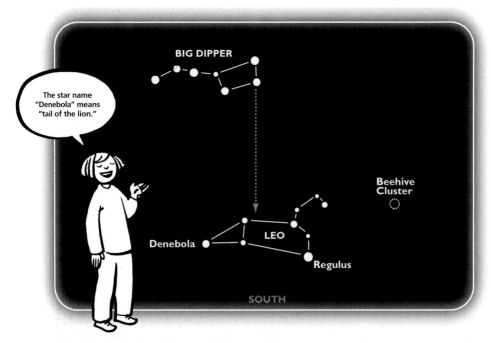

April and May are the best times to locate Leo, halfway up the southern sky. If you need help, look for the Big Dipper high overhead. Remember how the pointer stars in the bowl of the Big Dipper aim at Polaris? They also point in the opposite direction, right at the back of the lion.

LEO, THE LION

In ancient Egyptian times, lions ranged over huge territories and were both respected and feared by humans. The constellation known to us as Leo was also a lion in Egyptian sky lore. This constellation was very important to the ancient Egyptians, since the Sun passed through it every June when the Nile River was in flood. People imagined the cosmic king of beasts joining his strength with that of the Sun god, Ra, to create the blazing summer heat.

 Best time to look: April through early June.
See Spring Star Chart.

LOOK IN THE HANDBOOK

That lion had better watch out, because he's stalking a beehive — more specifically, the Beehive star cluster. For a closer look, see page 23 of the *Observer's Handbook*.

SPRING INTO SUMMER

The appearance of two bright stars — Arcturus, 37 light-years distant, and Spica, 260 light-years distant — signals that summer is on the way. Arcturus is the brightest star in the spring sky. It is located in the relatively simple star pattern of **Bootes**, the Herdsman. To one side of Bootes is the little constellation of **Corona Borealis**, the Northern Crown.

Spica, residing in the constellation of **Virgo**, the Maiden, is only a little dimmer than Arcturus, despite its much greater distance from us. Though Spica is fairly isolated in the sky, it is in a constellation of the zodiac and therefore competes for attention with the bright planets that wander lazily past it from time to time. Virgo is a difficult pattern to recognize — even with vivid Spica as a guide. The hologram on page 28 will help.

KNOWING THEIR NAMES

Arcturus (ark-TOUR-us)
Bootes (bo-OH-teez)
Corona Borealis (kor-OH-nah bo-ree-ALICE)
Spica (SPIKE-ah)
Virgo (VURR-go)

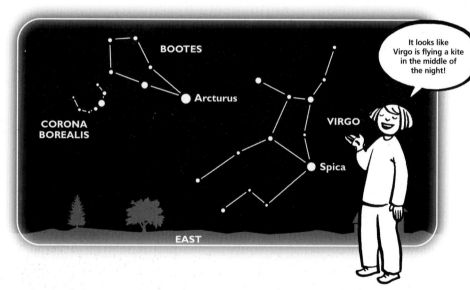

It looks like Virgo is flying a kite in the middle of the night!

The name Bootes has nothing to do with footwear. According to legend, Bootes was a herdsman, a shape you won't recognize here. The stars of Bootes do form a very fine kite, with orangey Arcturus at the bottom helping to mark the kite's tail. Another simple shape to pick out is the crown of neighboring Corona Borealis.

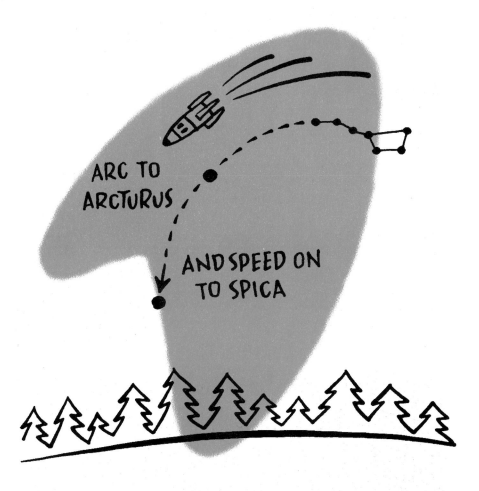

ARC TO
ARCTURUS

AND SPEED ON
TO SPICA

The stars in the Big Dipper's handle curve southward toward Arcturus and Spica. To help you find them, just remember the old saying, "Follow the Arc to Arcturus, and Speed on to Spica."

LOOK IN THE HANDBOOK

Did you know that the stars shine with different colors, and that you can actually see those colors with just an ordinary pair of binoculars? See page 16 of the *Observer's Handbook* to learn more about the colors of Arcturus, Spica, and other stars.

VIRGO, THE MAIDEN

Virgo was a Greek goddess associated with agriculture. Her constellation becomes prominent in spring when the grain is planted and disappears in late summer when the time for the harvest approaches. One of the many Greek stories about Virgo casts her in the role of Erigone, the loving daughter of the winemaker Icarius. When her father was fatally injured, Erigone died of grief, on the spot. The gods took pity on both of them and carried the father and daughter to the stars. There, Erigone was transformed into Virgo, and Icarius became Bootes.

 Best time to look: May through July. See Spring Star Chart.

THE MILKY WAY

In Chinese sky lore, the Milky Way was the Celestial River, along whose banks sprawled the estate of the Chinese Sun god. One day, the Sun god's daughter, the Weaving Princess, spotted her father's handsome cowherd tending his cattle. She fell in love with him, and they were soon married. Unfortunately, the two lovers neglected their royal duties. The Sun god banished them to opposite sides of the river. The unhappy couple were allowed to meet only on the seventh day of the seventh month of each year. It was decreed that, on that day, all the magpies in China should fly to the river and form a bridge for the pair to cross. The stars Vega (the Weaving Princess) and Altair (the cowherd) [see next page] appear on different sides of the Milky Way. Albireo, a star 385 light-years away, appears midway between them. It symbolizes the first magpie arriving at the Celestial River to form the bridge.

Chinese sky lore also explained why the Milky Way disappears in moonlight. The Milky Way — the Celestial River — is filled with luminous silver fish. When the crescent Moon appears near the Milky Way, the frightened fish dive to the river bottom, because the Moon looks like a fish-hook.

 **Best time to look: July through September.
See Summer Star Chart.**

THE SUMMER TRIANGLE

T he **Summer Triangle** gives you three constellations for the price of one. Three brilliant stars outline a huge triangle that rides high in the southern sky all through summer and into autumn. The three stars are Vega, 25 light-years distant, Altair, almost 17 light-years distant, and Deneb, a whopping 1,600 light-years away. Deneb has to shine a lot harder than the other two stars to illuminate its corner of the Summer Triangle.

Each of these stars is also the main star in a constellation. Vega dominates tiny **Lyra**, the Harp. Altair is the gleaming eye of **Aquila**, the Eagle. Deneb is the tail of **Cygnus**, the Swan.

Making out two birds and a harp among these stars is a challenge. If you have trouble, try spotting a tiny, squashed square in Lyra. Aquila's stars form a much bigger diamond shape. Cygnus is often called the Northern Cross because of its shape. The band of the Milky Way, like a river, runs right through it.

Wait until you are in the country to look for the splendid but faint constellation of **Hercules**, located one third of the way from Vega to Arcturus. Hercules was a legendary Greek hero and the strongest man in the world. His strength and persistence saw him through the arduous Twelve Labors of Hercules, a test of endurance assigned by the gods that eventually won Hercules immortality among the stars.

KNOWING THEIR NAMES

Albireo (al-BEER-ee-oh)
Altair (al-TAIR)
Aquila (A-quill-ah)
Cygnus (SIG-nus)
Delta (DELL-tah)
Deneb (DEN-eb)
Epsilon (EPP-sih-lon)
Hercules (HER-cue-leez)
Lyra (LYE-rah)
Vega (VAY-gah, or VEE-gah)

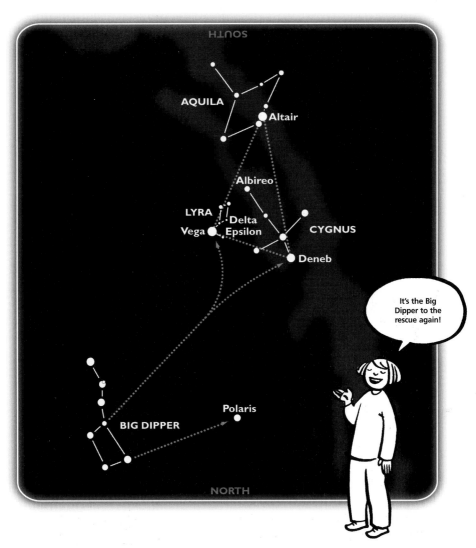

Having trouble finding the Summer Triangle? Recall that the pointer stars in the bowl of the Big Dipper point to Polaris. In early summer, the other two stars in the Big Dipper's bowl aim above the North Star and point roughly to the Summer Triangle.

✦ ⋆ LOOK IN THE HANDBOOK ⋆

The double stars Epsilon and Delta, both in Lyra, are great targets for your binoculars. See page 19 of the *Observer's Handbook*.

THE ARCHER AND THE SCORPION

According to Greek legend, **Sagittarius** was an Archer in pursuit of **Scorpius**, the poisonous Scorpion. Scorpius is fun to trace. Begin with his head of three stars in a row. Continue through his heart, marked by bright, reddish Antares, roughly 600 light-years away. Antares means "rival of Mars" — the red-hued planet occasionally drifts nearby. Below Antares, follow the scorpion's fish-hook tail to where it ends at a pair of stars. The brighter star, about 700 light-years away, is called Shaula, which means "sting."

KNOWING THEIR
NAMES

Antares (an-TAIR-eez)
Sagittarius (saj-ih-TAIR-ee-us)
Scorpius (SKOR-pee-us)
Shaula (SHOAL-ah)

The tail of the scorpion may or may not be visible, depending on where you live. In the southern United States, you can see it rise well above the south horizon. Those living near the international border in the eastern United States and Canada might see the tail resting right on the horizon. For those living above latitude 45 degrees north, the scorpion's tail is cut off altogether.

Today, Sagittarius is often called the **Teapot**, because a stick-figure outline of its eight brightest stars forms a pot, handle, and spout.

Those who live away from city lights can see the Milky Way make a glittering backdrop behind Scorpius and Sagittarius. Look for the Teapot — the Milky Way rises like steam from its spout. In the Scorpius Hologram on page 34, you can see a portion of the Milky Way as it appears in long-exposure photographs. See p.34

★ ★ LOOK IN THE HANDBOOK ★

You're in for a sky full of celestial treats if you explore the band of the Milky Way near Sagittarius and Scorpius with binoculars. See "Scanning the Milky Way" and "The Lagoon Nebula" on pages 24–26 of the *Observer's Handbook*.

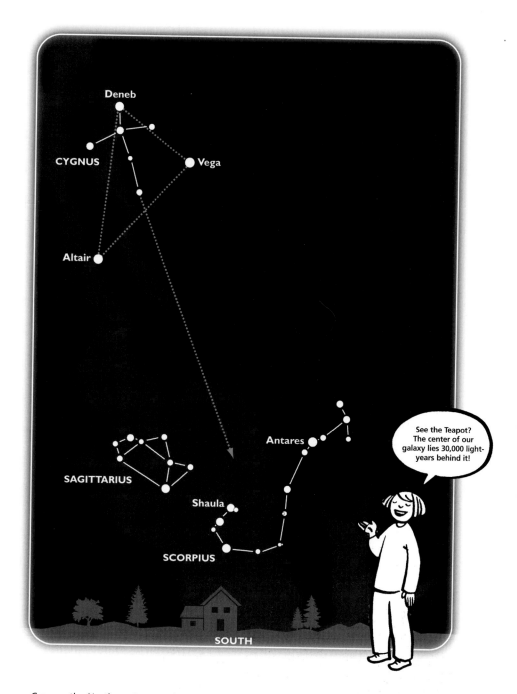

Cygnus, the Northern Cross, points southward, along the band of the Milky Way, to Scorpius. The visibility of the scorpion's tail depends on your latitude. This chart depicts the view at about latitude 40° north. Where you live, how much of the tail can you see?

SCORPIUS, THE SCORPION

As a favor to the Earth goddess, Gaia, Scorpius fatally stung the hunter Orion (find out why on page 39). He was rewarded with a home in the sky, but it turned out to be next door to militant Sagittarius, the Archer, who was determined to avenge Orion's death. The archer slew Scorpius with a single arrow. Sagittarius was a centaur, a special class of creature in Greek legend. A centaur boasted the head and shoulders of an athletic man and the body and legs of a horse. With a clear sky and a little imagination, you can picture the centaur-archer stalking his quarry, his bow and arrow aimed with deadly precision at the scorpion's heart.

 Best time to look: July and August.
See Summer Star Chart.

PEGASUS, THE WINGED HORSE

The constellation Pegasus has no hindquarters and no rider — and it glides upside down. Still, the flying horse was a majestic creature in Greek mythology.

Pearl-white Pegasus inherited his flying apparatus from the snake-infested, winged Medusa (don't ask how). The gentle steed put his wings to good use. He was the magical horse that the hero Perseus flew on to save Andromeda, daughter of King Cepheus and Queen Cassiopeia, from a giant sea monster called Cetus. All of these characters, except Medusa, are constellations in the autumn sky.

 **Best time to look: October through January.
See Autumn Star Chart.**

THE AUTUMN SQUARE

FROM THE GREAT SQUARE...

The autumn sky has few bright stars. Though many of its constellations are large, their shapes are dim and indistinct. The main exception is **Pegasus**, whose four central stars are comparable to Polaris in brightness and form a huge box. Pegasus was a flying horse in ancient Greek mythology. Modern sky charts usually label the box as the **Great Square** of Pegasus.

Watch the Great Square soon after it rises. It makes a great baseball diamond. The star nearest the horizon is home plate. The other corners of the Great Square mark first, second, and third base. If you really stretch your imagination, you might find a shortstop and some outfielders — but the pitcher and catcher seem to be hiding in the dugout.

> KNOWING THEIR
> ## NaMES
> ....
> **Andromeda**
> *(an-DROM-eh-duh)*
> **Pegasus** *(PEG-uh-sus)*

TO THE GREAT GALAXY

Neighboring **Andromeda**, the daughter of King Cepheus and Queen Cassiopeia, is one of many autumn constellations with no distinctive shape. However, it contains an amazing object known as the Andromeda Galaxy — or simply the Great Galaxy — the most distant object in the universe that can be glimpsed with the naked eye.

> ✱ ✱ LOOK IN THE HANDBOOK ✱
>
> **For instructions on how to locate the Andromeda Galaxy, see page 28 of the *Observer's Handbook*.**

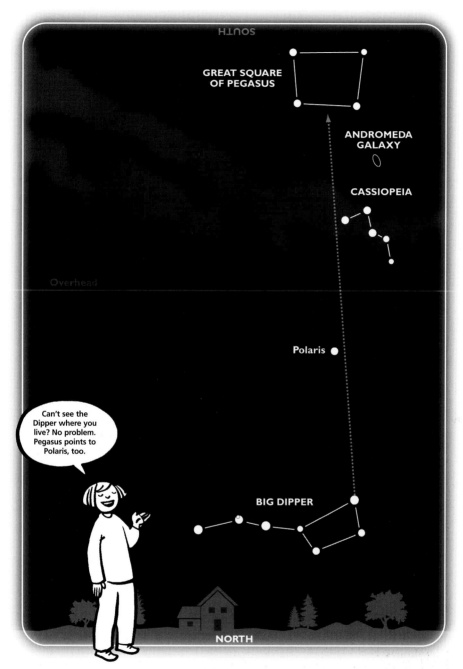

The Big Dipper scrapes the northern horizon each autumn. The pointer stars aim at Polaris. An equal distance above Polaris, near the sky's zenith, is the W or M of Cassiopeia. If you direct your gaze a bit past Cassiopeia, into the high southern sky, you'll come to the Great Square. Between the Square and the W is the smudge-like Andromeda Galaxy.

HUNTER ABOVE THE SNOW

Perhaps the greatest constellation of all is mighty **Orion**, the Hunter. When Orion is due south, he is well above the horizon and dominates the star groups around him. Orion is the key to finding all the less distinctive winter constellations.

The hunter has four bright stars to mark his broad shoulders and legs. The two best are bluish-white Rigel and reddish-orange Betelgeuse. Both of these stars look equally bright to us, yet Rigel, 770 light-years away, is almost twice as distant as Betelgeuse.

The three stars in a row that mark Orion's belt point to two other brilliant stars in the winter sky. Slide down the belt to find Sirius, brightest star in all the heavens. It should be. It's less than nine light-years away. Aim up along the belt to see Aldebaran, a reddish star 65 light-years distant.

Orion's head is marked by a small triangle of stars. Additional faint stars outline his club and shield, upraised as if ready for battle. Tucked below Orion's belt is his sword, composed of two faint stars and an even dimmer, fuzzy-looking star between them. The hazy patch in the sword is the Orion Nebula, one of the night sky's greatest treasures.

<aside>
KNOWING THEIR
NaMES

Orion (oh-RYE-un)
Aldebaran (al-DEB-uh-ran)
Betelgeuse (BET-el-jews)
Rigel (RYE-jel)
Sirius (SEAR-ee-us)
</aside>

ORION · Aldebaran · Betelgeuse · Rigel · Sirius · □ Orion Nebula · SOUTH

S K Y   M Y T H

ORION, THE HUNTER

Orion was a tower of strength, but ruthless and vain to the core. According to Greek legend, the mighty hunter boasted that he was superior to the gods and would run amok in the wilderness, crushing all living creatures. Gaia, Goddess of Earth, was not amused. She dispatched Scorpius, the poisonous scorpion, to fatally sting Orion. Later, she placed Orion and Scorpius in the heavens as constellations, but on opposite sides of the sky so that they could never tangle again.

 Best time to look: January through March.
See Winter Star Chart.

THE WINTER CIRCLE

Have you noticed how the sky on a cold winter's night seems ablaze with brilliant stars? The part of the sky we see in winter holds more bright stars than the parts seen at other times of the year. Many of these bright stars are arranged in a huge **Winter Circle** that is easy to trace.

Start off with the sparkling star Rigel in the constellation Orion. As we've seen, Orion's belt points to the stars Sirius and Aldebaran. The other four stars of the Winter Circle are brilliant Capella, which rides high overhead all winter long, Castor and Pollux, known as the Twins, and Procyon. These four range from 11 to 45 light-years away, one reason why the Winter Circle gleams.

These stars adorn five constellations gathered around Orion. Capella is on the roof of the house-shaped **Auriga**, the Chariot Driver. Castor and Pollux are the two faces of **Gemini**, the Twins. Procyon blazes out from tiny **Canis Minor**, the Little Dog. Sirius marks the nose of **Canis Major**, the Big Dog. Aldebaran is the blood-red eye of **Taurus**, the Bull.

These constellations are less distinctive than Orion, so don't feel badly if you can't identify them right away. In the top half of the Winter Circle, beware of planets masquerading as stars. For example, from autumn 2000 to spring 2002, Jupiter and Saturn will drift through Taurus and Gemini. Learn more about the planets in the next section of this book.

KNOWING THEIR NAMES

Auriga (oh-RYE-gah)
Canis Major (KAY-niss MAY-jer)
Canis Minor (KAY-niss My-ner)
Capella (kah-PELL-ah)
Castor (KAS-ter)
Gemini (GEM-in-eye)
Hyades (HI-a-deez)
Pleiades (PLEE-ah-deez)
Pollux (PAW-lux)
Procyon (PRO-see-on)
Taurus (TOR-us)

✶ LOOK IN THE HANDBOOK ✶

The sky's finest star cluster, the Pleiades, is located near the Winter Circle. A second cluster, the Hyades, is right on the Circle. To view them, see pages 20–21 of the *Observer's Handbook*.

Just below Orion's belt is the great Orion Nebula, a place where stars are made. See page 27 of the *Observer's Handbook*. ✶

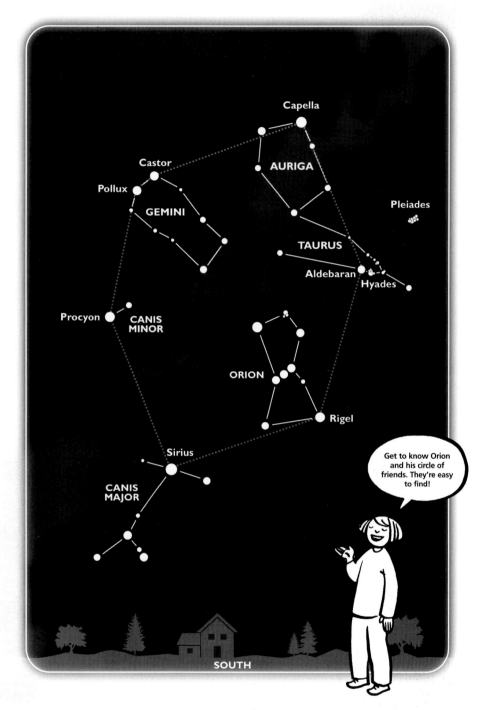

The Winter Circle joins six constellations. They're sometimes known as the Winter Six.

THE SOLAR SYSTEM—IN ACTION

Our solar system contains the Sun, the nine planets that orbit it, and a multitude of smaller objects — moons, asteroids, and comets. The planets' journeys around the Sun never stop, and their positions in the night sky are always changing. In fact, the word "planet" comes from the Greek word for "wanderer."

However, the planets don't wander anywhere they like. Imagine a flat surface in space, like an invisible, almost circular racecourse. The Sun sits at the center of this imaginary racecourse, and the planets are the runners, each with its own track. Now imagine the planets racing around the Sun. Planets on the inside tracks finish sooner because they have less distance to travel. Also, the inner planets orbit faster, because they feel the Sun's gravity more than the outer planets do. Like our imaginary racecourse, the solar system is essentially flat. A flat surface or space is called a *plane*.

THE SUN'S PATH

Earth is tilted on its axis. As our planet circles the Sun once each year, for a few months the top leans toward the Sun and the bottom away from it. It is warmer in the north and cooler in the south. Half a year later, when Earth has traveled to the other side of the Sun, the same tilt causes the south to get warm and the north to get cold. In other words, Earth's tilt causes the seasons. Because of that tilt, the Sun appears high overhead in summer and closer to the horizon in winter. As the months pass, the Sun inches eastward through the sky. Over a year, the Sun's changing position traces an S-shaped curve, called the *ecliptic*. The ecliptic is also the center of the pathway followed by the Moon and planets. Because the orbits of the planets — and the Moon — all lie almost on the same plane, we always see them drifting along the same part of the sky — near the ecliptic.

The orbital speeds of the inner planets are faster than those of the outer planets. All of the planets would fly off into space if it weren't for the pull of the Sun's gravity.

Because the orbits of the planets all lie roughly on one plane, the planets appear to drift along a narrow pathway in the sky. Slow or fast, the planets trace out virtually the same invisible paths over and over, year after year. Unlike the runners in a race, though, the planets are never all lined up in a row. Their orbits carry them far apart in space, though sometimes they pass one another on their journeys.

THE SOLAR SYSTEM FAMILY

The planets come in two groups. The first, called the *terrestrial planets*, is composed of dense, rocky worlds that closely orbit the Sun. Mercury, Venus, Earth, and Mars are in this group. The terrestrial planets complete their orbits very quickly, in less than one or two Earth years. Venus is easily the brightest planet in our sky.

KNOWING THEIR
NaMES
....
Charon (CAR-on)

The second group, the *giant planets*, consists of Jupiter, Saturn, Uranus, and Neptune. These are much bigger planets that orbit the Sun from much farther away. It takes many years for them to complete their orbits. Made mostly of light, colorless gases, these planets have lots of moons and rings. Jupiter is the brightest member of the giant planets.

Frigid Pluto doesn't fit in either set. It is smaller than any terrestrial planet and almost as lightweight as the giant planets. Pluto and its moon, Charon, remain a mystery to be explored in the 21st century.

THE ZODIAC ZONE

Like kids delivering newspapers, planets are always on the go, but they follow the same route. A special band of 12 constellations marks the pathway of the planets. We call this band the zodiac.

You've already met Aquarius, Leo, Virgo, Scorpius, Sagittarius, Gemini, and Taurus. The other zodiac constellations are: **Capricornus**, the Goat; **Pisces**, the Fish; **Aries**, the Ram; **Cancer**, the Crab; and **Libra**, the Scales.

You don't need to know all the zodiac constellations to qualify as an expert planet-finder. Only a few bright stars in the zodiac zone can be mistaken for planets.

Most of the zodiac star-patterns are not distinctive. Anything you see in the zodiac's fainter regions that *looks* like a bright star is sure to be a planet.

Some planets might be in the Sun's glare when you want to see them. Others might be rising after midnight when you are asleep. But the planets are always moving. Before long, a bright one will appear, somewhere along the zodiac, at a convenient hour.

KNOWING THEIR NAMES

Aquarius (a-QUAIR-ee-us)
Aries (AIR-eez)
Cancer (CAN-sir)
Capricornus (kap-ri-KOR-nus)
Fomalhaut (FOAM-a-lot)
Libra (LEE-bra)
Pisces (PIE-sees)

PISCES

JUPITER

★ ★ LOOK IN THE HANDBOOK ★

To find the best time of year to look for each of the constellations of the zodiac, check the "Constellation Club" log on pages 30–31 of the *Observer's Handbook.*

PLANETS IN A CRYSTAL BALL

For the ancients, the Sun — upon whose light all life on our planet depends — was the most important object in the sky. They knew that the Moon and planets travel near the path that the Sun travels by day — the ecliptic. Because the part of the sky the Sun passed through was so special to the ancients, they made up the band of constellations we call the zodiac.

To the astronomer-priests of antiquity, the bright, wandering planets symbolized heavenly powers that could influence people and events. The art of astrology developed from these ancient beliefs. Even today, astrologers try to predict human affairs from the changing positions of the Sun, Moon, and planets. However, astrology has no scientific basis. Earth is not the focus of planetary motion, and planets don't foretell the future — they are simply remote worlds in outer space.

The zodiac forms the beltway traveled by the Sun, Moon, and planets. The stars in the section of the zodiac occupied by Pisces, Aquarius, and Capricornus are not very bright, so any planets there should stand out. However, don't be fooled by the first-magnitude star Fomalhaut, 25 light-years away, which lies south of Aquarius, just outside the zodiac zone.

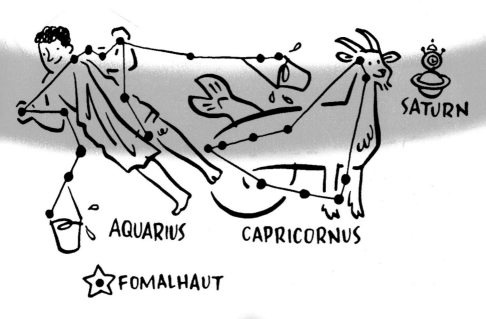

SATURN

AQUARIUS

CAPRICORNUS

FOMALHAUT

THE PLANETS

PLANETS YOU CAN SEE

Unlike stars, planets do not make their own light. The light of the Sun reflects, or bounces, off their surfaces and back to us on Earth. Of the eight planets besides Earth, five are visible to the naked eye. They are Mercury, Venus, Mars, Jupiter, and Saturn.

The planets are constantly moving among the constellations. This is especially true of the twilight speedsters, Mercury and Venus. The Fact File on page 49 will help you to locate slower-moving Mars, Jupiter, and Saturn.

You can get up-to-date positions for all the planets from an observatory or planetarium. Monthly astronomy magazines chart the planets on star maps and are available at most newsstands and public libraries. The Internet is another good place to find this information. Some web sites are suggested on page 60.

MERCURY

MERCURY AND VENUS
Horizon Huggers

Mercury and Venus, orbiting close to the Sun, never appear far from the Sun in our sky. They sink into the western horizon an hour or two after sunset or rise in the east at dawn. They are prisoners of twilight.

Mercury is the closest to the Sun and the most difficult of the visible planets to see. Use binoculars to find its solitary dot of light in the

F A C T F I L E	Mercury	Venus	Earth
Diameter	3,000 miles (4900 km)	7,600 miles (12 100 km)	7,900 miles (12 800 km)
Average distance from Sun	36 million miles (58 million km)	67.5 million miles (108 million km)	93 million miles (150 million km)
Distance if Earth = 1	0.4	0.7	1
Orbiting time	88 days	225 days	365.25 days
Orbital speed	29.8 mps (47.7 kps)	22 mps (35.2 kps)	18 mps (29.6 kps)
Known moons	0	0	1

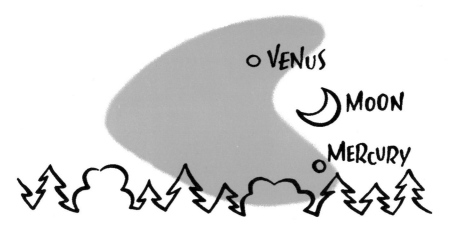

Venus

Moon

Mercury

Gleaming Venus often appears above the treetops, but Mercury is much fainter and always hugs the horizon. The crescent Moon occasionally glides near these planets, making them easier to identify.

twilight sky. Venus gets closer to us than does any other planet. This Earth-sized world reflects a lot of sunlight, because it is cloaked in a blanket of cloud. Though it rises or sets within a few hours of the Sun, brilliant Venus easily pierces the twilight. Occasionally, Venus is visible for a brief time just before twilight begins in the morning or after it ends in the evening

VENUS

PLANET-WATCHING TIPS

① **Planets are bright.** Planets are much smaller than stars, but much closer to us. Jupiter and Venus always look brighter than any star. So does Mars when it is closest to Earth. Saturn is comparable to stars such as Vega and Capella. Mercury is a bright light, too, but it must always compete with the glare of twilight.

② **Planets are steady.** We see the stars as twinkling points of light. Because the planets are so much nearer to us, their light enters our atmosphere in a beam that withstands turbulence in the air. Thus, planets do not twinkle, they shine with a steady glow — except when they are near the horizon, where we see them through more air.

③ **Planets are wanderers.** Remember, planets have motions separate from the stars. They drift slowly through the sky against the backdrop of constellations.

MARS
The Every-Other-Year Planet

Mars is known as the Red Planet. Its iron-rich soil has a red hue, making Mars glow with a red tint in the sky. Mars has virtually no cloud cover, so

MARS

it reflects less light than Venus does. It's also only half the size of Venus. Still, when Mars is closest to Earth in its orbit, it shines brighter than any star. But Mars and Earth play a game of tag in their orbits. It takes about 26 months for the two planets to line up again. You can expect Mars to be a bright sky-object only every second year. Fortunately, Mars is not confined to twilight.

When it is closest to us, it rises in the east roughly when the Sun sets in the west. For a few weeks, Mars is visible for the entire night. For help in locating Mars, see the Fact File on the next page.

JUPITER AND SATURN
Old Reliables

Jupiter, the largest planet in the solar system, shines brilliant white and completes an orbit around the Sun in almost 12 years. This means that Jupiter spends about one year in each of the 12 constellations of the zodiac.

JUPITER

Glowing a yellowish color, Saturn is the most distant planet visible to the eye. It takes nearly 30 years to orbit the Sun, spending two years or more in each zodiac

---

F A C T   F I L E

	Mars	**Jupiter**	**Saturn**
Diameter	4,200 miles	89,000 miles	75,300 miles
	(6800 km)	(143 000 km)	(120 500 km)
Average distance from Sun	142 million miles	486 million miles	890 million miles
	(228 million km)	(778 million km)	(1.4 billion km)
Distance if Earth = 1	1.5	5.2	9.5
Orbiting time	687 days	11.86 years	29.46 years
Orbital speed	15 mps (24 kps)	8.1 mps (13 kps)	6 mps (9.6 kps)
Known moons	2	16	18

constellation. Saturn's famous rings are made of icy chunks of various sizes in orbit around the planet.

SATURN

Every year, Jupiter and Saturn become prominent evening objects for several months. Once you have identified these slow but dependable fellows, you can easily keep track of them for the rest of your life. Check the Fact File below to determine where Jupiter and Saturn are currently residing. You may even be able to see one of them tonight.

F A C T   F I L E

Where to Find Them

Here's where to find Mars, Jupiter, and Saturn in 1999–2010. (Mars is listed only for years and months in which it comes closest to Earth.) The "Constellation Club" log on pages 30–31 of the *Observer's Handbook* lists the season in which each constellation is visible.

	Mars	*Jupiter*	*Saturn*
1999	Virgo (April–May)	Pisces–Aries	Aries
2000		Taurus	Taurus
2001	Scorpius (June)	Taurus–Gemini	Taurus
2002		Gemini	Taurus
2003	Aquarius (September)	Cancer	Taurus–Gemini
2004		Leo	Gemini
2005	Aries (November)	Virgo	Gemini
2006		Libra	Cancer
2007	Gemini (December)	Scorpius	Leo
2008	Gemini (January)	Sagittarius	Leo
2009		Capricornus	Leo–Virgo
2010	Cancer (February)	Aquarius	Virgo

★ ★ LOOK IN THE HANDBOOK ★

Seeing the moons of other planets requires a telescope — except in the case of Jupiter. With only binoculars, you can spot the four moons (of Jupiter's 16) that Galileo discovered nearly 400 years ago. For details, see "The Moons of Jupiter" on page 14 of the *Observer's Handbook*.

URANUS

NEPTUNE

PLUTO

BEYOND SATURN
The "Invisible" Planets

The solar system's three most distant planets are invisible to sky watchers who don't use telescopes.

Uranus was accidentally discovered in 1781 by an astronomer using a small telescope. Neptune was found in 1846 after astronomers used mathematical calculations to pinpoint its position in the sky. Pluto, the planet whose orbit takes it farthest from the Sun, was discovered in 1930 after many years of scanning for a suspected Planet X.

Is there another planet past Pluto? The gravity of such an object would pull Neptune and Pluto slightly out of position, and astronomers think they would have detected that effect by now. Recently, however, astronomers have discovered numerous small, icy objects in a broad zone beyond Pluto. It is just possible that an undetected Pluto-sized iceberg lurks in the void far, far beyond Pluto.

FACT FILE

	Uranus	Neptune	Pluto
Diameter	32,000 miles	31,000 miles	1,400 miles
	(51 100 km)	(49 500 km)	(2300 km)
Average distance from Sun	1.8 billion miles	2.8 billion miles	3.7 billion miles
	(2.9 billion km)	(4.5 billion km)	(5.9 billion km)
Distance if Earth = 1	19.2	30.1	40 approx.
Orbiting time	84 years	165 years	248 years
Orbital speed	4.2 mps (6.7 kps)	3.4 mps (5.4 kps)	2.9 mps (4.6 kps)
Known moons	17	8	1

WHAT'S IN A NAME?

The people who first named the planets are unknown to us. The names we use today are those of gods in Roman mythology. Mercury, the fastest-moving planet, was the messenger of the gods. Venus, so lovely in the twilight sky, was the goddess of love and beauty. Blood-red Mars was the war god. Jupiter, brightest "star" in the midnight sky and the largest planet, was king of the gods. The slowest planet visible to the eye is named after the Roman god Saturn, also known as Cronus, the Greek name for the god of time.

Uranus, Neptune, and Pluto were discovered in relatively recent times, but their discoverers followed the tradition of naming planets after figures in Roman mythology. Uranus was the first sky god and the father of Saturn. Neptune was the god of the sea and a brother of Jupiter. And Pluto — a world isolated at the fringe of the solar system — was another of Jupiter's brothers and the god of the underworld and the dead.

VENUS

MARS

PHASES OF THE MOON

The Moon is Earth's natural satellite and closest neighbor. It is only one-quarter the diameter of Earth. It orbits Earth every 27 and a third days — a few days short of one calendar month. As the Moon travels around Earth, it glides completely around the sky, changing its position and shape as it goes. The Moon's changing shapes are called *phases*. They occur because the Moon has no light of its own. It only reflects light from the Sun.

At the phase of the Moon called *new Moon*, the Moon and Sun set together in the west. The Moon is invisible, because sunlight is illuminating the side of the Moon facing totally away from us. As it moves eastward in its orbit, the Moon becomes visible for longer and longer periods.

A night or two after new Moon, a slim *crescent Moon* appears in the evening twilight. Night after night, the Moon grows fatter. At *first quarter*, the Moon is shaped like half a pie, because half of the side facing us is in sunlight. A first-quarter Moon is visible for roughly half the night.

After first quarter, the Moon continues to bulge more and more, and this Moon is called a *gibbous Moon* ("gibbous" means "convex," or "bulging," on both sides). About a week after first quarter, sunlight fills the side of the Moon that faces us, forming a *full Moon*. A full Moon rises in the east as the Sun sets in the west. It is visible for the entire night.

In the nights following full Moon, the phases peel away in the opposite order. The Moon is seen for shorter and shorter portions of the night. Once past *last quarter*, the Moon does not rise until well after midnight.

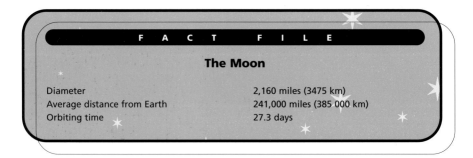

F A C T   F I L E

The Moon

Diameter	2,160 miles (3475 km)
Average distance from Earth	241,000 miles (385 000 km)
Orbiting time	27.3 days

During the fourth week of the month, the Moon again thins to a crescent and then becomes lost in morning twilight.

Soon it is new Moon again. The Sun and Moon are once more close to each other in the sky, and a *lunar month* has been completed.

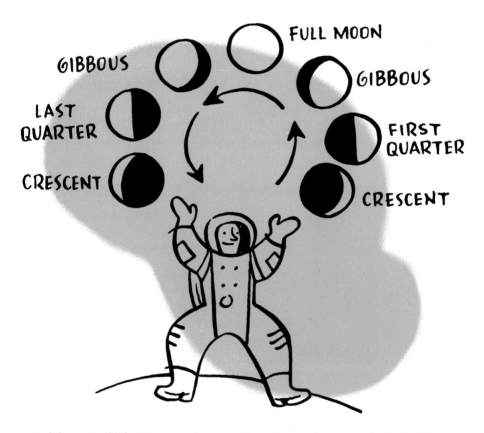

Each lunar month, the Moon goes from new Moon through first quarter during the first week, to full Moon in the second week, to last quarter in the third week, then back to new Moon by the end of the fourth week.

LOOK IN THE HANDBOOK

Find Moon-gazing activities on pages 8-13 of the *Observer's Handbook.*

SATELLITES ARE A CINCH

Thousands of Earth-orbiting spacecraft are hard at work, 24 hours a day, studying space beyond and Earth below. Their many jobs include transmitting television signals, gathering information about Earth's resources, and helping to predict the weather. A sampling of these *artificial satellites* crisscrosses the sky every night. Satellites look like ordinary stars adrift among the constellations. Keep your eyes peeled, because satellites appear anywhere, move in any direction, and take only a minute or so to drift across the entire sky.

We see satellites purely by reflected sunlight. If the spacecraft is tumbling or spinning, sunlight might glint off various shiny components, causing the dot of light in the sky to pulsate or even blink on and off. If the light disappears, it may be because the satellite has drifted into Earth's shadow. Bigger space-craft, such as the Space Shuttle, are the easiest to spot. When the International Space Station is completed, it will gleam more brightly than any star.

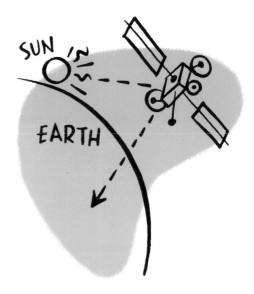

The best time to look for satellites is during the first — or last — hours of the night, when the Sun is not far below the horizon. Then the orbiting spacecraft are in their best positions to reflect sunlight down to us. City stargazers will see only the brighter satellites, but just keep looking. You are sure to spot one sooner or later.

Stars that drift out of place are probably artificial satellites. Be careful not to confuse satellites with jet planes, though. Airplanes usually give themselves away with their flashing strobe lights.

COMETS: ICEBERGS IN SPACE

There is a huge number of comets in the solar system, but you won't see many without a telescope. Comets are mountain-sized, frozen balls of gas and dust that begin their lives in an enormous bank of comets surrounding the solar system. The Sun's gravity pulls in a steady stream of these cosmic icebergs. They drift sunward for months, curve around the Sun in a matter of weeks, then shoot back beyond Pluto, usually not to be seen again for thousands of years, if ever.

As a comet enters the inner solar system, the Sun warms the comet's frozen center until an envelope of gas glows all around it. The vaporized gas and dust then flow away from the comet in a long, ghostly tail that can be millions of miles long — and so thin you can see right through it.

With the help of telescopes, astronomers see a dozen or more comets every year. Every few years, a comet comes close enough to be seen with binoculars — if sky conditions are good enough. There is not usually much advance warning, unless the comet is very bright. In early 1997, newspapers and television gave lots of attention to Comet Hale-Bopp, a very fine comet visible to the unaided eye that spring.

★ HAIRY STARS

The word "comet" means "hairy star." Until the last century or so, hairy stars were considered bad omens. The unpredicted arrival of a comet would disrupt the perfection of the heavens. Sometimes adrift among the constellations for weeks, hairy stars were viewed as ugly intruders. Comets throughout history were blamed for wars, famines, plagues, and other natural disasters. In 1910, Earth passed through the tail of Halley's Comet, which visits us every 76 years. Some people worried that our atmosphere would trap poisonous cometary vapors. Hustlers sold phony "comet pills" to those gullible enough to buy them. Today, comets enjoy a better reputation. Their visits are celebrated as rare, stunningly beautiful sights.

CATCH A FALLING STAR

We know the stars don't fall, but rocks do — rocks from outer space. They shoot through the atmosphere and burn up in a flash of light. You will need patience to see them. A falling star is more properly called a meteor. Like satellites, meteors can appear at any time, anywhere in the sky. Unlike satellites, they usually flash for only a second or two before vanishing. On rare occasions, a brilliant meteor slices across the sky, leaving a brief tail in its wake. Only

TRICKY TERMS

A small rock or pebble in interplanetary space is called a *meteoroid.* If a meteoroid falls into Earth's atmosphere, it burns up in a flash of light called a *meteor.* If the rock is big enough, it might survive its fiery plunge to the ground. Then it is called a *meteorite.*

a few meteors are visible each hour — and only if you are scanning the sky carefully from a country location. Meteors are difficult to see in the illuminated skies above towns and cities.

The best time to watch for meteors is during a *meteor shower*. A meteor shower occurs when Earth intersects the orbital pathway of an icy comet. Small particles of dust and ice from the comet's tail are strewn along the comet's pathway. When Earth plows through this cometary debris, meteor activity really picks up.

The best meteor shower of the year occurs each August when Earth travels through an especially dense belt of comet material. The shower is named the Perseids, because the meteors radiate from a point inside the constellation of **Perseus**, the heroic rescuer of Andromeda. When the shower reaches its peak on August 11 or 12, look up in any direction — perhaps from a cottage or campground where skies are dark — and you might see three or four dozen meteors per *hour*.

KNOWING THEIR

NAMES

Perseus *(PURR-see-us)*
Perseids *(PURR-see-idz)*

10
TIPS FOR A
SUCCESSFUL METEOR WATCH

1 Get as far away as possible from tall buildings and streetlights.

2 It gets chilly at night, so dress warmly — and don't forget to bring bug spray.

3 Bring a flashlight in case you need it, but don't shine it needlessly or you will reduce your night vision.

4 For a deluxe sky watch, lie in a reclining lawn chair. Wrap yourself in a sleeping bag if you have one.

5 Don't stare in the direction of the Moon. Pick the darkest-looking part of the sky.

6 Try not to look down. Meteors flash by quickly.

7 Feel sleepy? Get up and walk around, then do some more observing.

8 Keep a count. The number of meteors usually increases as the night wears on.

9 If you are observing the Perseids, hold an outdoor sleepover, set your alarm for after midnight, and watch the shower at its strongest.

10 For safety's sake, ask your parents (and your friends) to join you. A group meteor watch is more fun.

THE NORTHERN LIGHTS

he northern lights are well named. You usually have to look north to find their shimmering colors, and the farther north you live, the more often you see them. The scientific name for the northern lights is *aurora borealis*, which means "lights of the north." An aurora often begins as a greenish-white arc glowing near the northern horizon. From the city, you might not even notice it. Even those living in the country can confuse the northern lights with the glow from a nearby city.

However, if the aurora is a good one, bright vertical spikes, or rays, will grow out of the glowing arc. The most active auroras turn the sky into pulsating sheets of all colors of the rainbow. Sometimes rippling streamers of pale color radiate from far overhead down to the horizon. Then the aurora can be seen in almost every part of the sky.

Auroras are difficult to predict. It's a good idea to check the sky for them every clear night.

5 TIPS FOR SPOTTING AN AURORA

1. You don't need a telescope to see an aurora, just your bare eyes.
2. When checking for a display, be sure to first look low in the north.
3. Analyze what you see. Is there a glow? What shape and color is it? Is it in motion?
4. Look for streaking rays. If they begin to slide sideways and change color, you are in for a superb aurora.
5. Some auroras disappear and return later. Check the sky from time to time for signs of activity.

NATURE'S LIGHT SHOW

cientific research indicates that there is a connection between auroras and *sunspots,* the dark patches that sometimes appear on the Sun's surface. When sunspots flare up, they release clouds of charged particles — electrified bits of matter — into space. If these particles reach Earth, they interact with our upper atmosphere, causing it to glow in different colors and create an aurora.

TELESCOPES AND BINOCULARS

All you really need for sky watching is this book and your own two eyes. Still, once you become interested in astronomy, it is only natural to want a telescope. Counting the craters of the Moon, inspecting Saturn's rings, and snaring distant galaxies are all exciting prospects. However, even small telescopes are expensive. Many come with complex mountings and controls that are difficult to figure out. Telescopes view only a tiny section of sky, so pointing them requires skill and patience. Then, if you magnify a planet or a star too much, it becomes fuzzy. These distortions are worse with cheap telescopes, which often claim to offer a level of magnification, or *power,* that is simply not attainable. This is disappointing, frustrating, and discouraging. You don't want that.

BINOCULARS — TELESCOPES IN STEREO

Binoculars are an excellent alternative to telescopes. They are easy to handle, give much wider views of the sky, and involve both your eyes. The sky objects described in the *Observer's Handbook* are excellent targets for those who want to see the sky a little more close-up.

Binoculars come in a variety of sizes and prices. Unlike cheap telescopes, which often come with wobbly mounts and poor lenses, inexpensive binoculars can be truly helpful in learning about the night sky. Keep in mind that binoculars are just as effective at revealing faint stars as are small telescopes, which can cost several hundred dollars.

STARGAZING IN CYBERSPACE

The Internet contains a wealth of information about astronomy, space missions, and skygazing, but the maze of links is sometimes bewildering. To get started, try these addresses on the web. A few of the sites are designed for young people. You'll soon find your way to many more astronomical subject areas. Begin each website address below by typing "http://" (without the quotation marks).

ASTRONOMY WEB SITES

• Don't miss the Griffith Observatory Star Awards. Each week, Griffith adds a new address to its list of award-winning web sites, including links to the Hubble Space Telescope and all major planetary missions.
StarAwards:
www.Griffithobs.org/StarAward.html

• The Planetary Society, in Pasadena, California, is dedicated to the exploration of space and the Search for Extraterrestrial Intelligence (SETI). Be sure to click on their "Young Explorers" link.
Planetary Society:
www.planetary.org

• These three web sites, designed especially for kids, contain lots of activities and special events, many of them on a space exploration theme.
Berit's Best Sites for Children: **db.cochran.com /li_showElems:theoPage:theo:3548:0.db**
Space Place:
spaceplace.jpl.nasa.gov/spacepl.htm

Space Day:
www.spaceday.com/

• If you are looking for more charts of the constellations, or if you want to keep track of the Moon and planets from month to month, visit these web sites.
Skywatcher's Diary:
www.pa.msu.edu/abrams/diary.html
Izzy's Skylog:
darkstar.swsc.k12.ar.us/~izzy
The Constellations and Their Stars:
www. astro.wisc.edu/~dolan/constellations/

• Astronomy clubs are a great way to meet other people interested in your hobby. These addresses for the two biggest astronomical societies in the US and Canada contain information on the club nearest to you.
Astronomical League:
www.astroleague.org
Royal Astronomical Society of Canada:
www.rasc.ca/

GLOSSARY

astronomy. the scientific study of celestial bodies, such as the stars and the planets.

atmosphere. the layer of gas that surrounds some moons and planets.

axis of Earth. an imaginary line connecting Earth's North and South Poles.

binary star. two stars that orbit each other.

celestial. of the sky or any object in outer space.

celestial poles. the North and South Poles of the sky sphere.

circumpolar stars / constellations. stars / constellations so close to one of the celestial poles that they never set below the horizon.

comet. a ball of dust and gas, usually frozen, that circles the sun in an extremely long orbit.

constellation. the pattern made by a group of stars in the sky.

cosmos. the universe.

crater. a hollow with a raised rim on the surface of a planet or moon, caused by the impact of a meteoroid or small asteroid.

diameter. the length of a straight line passing from one side of an object through the center of the object to the other side.

double star. two stars that appear very close together.

ecliptic. the imaginary pathway that the Sun follows each year through the constellations in the sky.

galaxy. a vast system of stars — much bigger than a star cluster — held together by gravity.

Galileo. a great Italian astronomer of the early 17th century.

gas. a form of matter that has no particular shape and can expand to fill any available container or space.

gravity. the force that pulls objects toward each other. Bigger, more massive objects pull harder. The Sun's gravity keeps the planets in their orbits.

The Great Square. four stars forming a big box in the constellation Pegasus.

horizon. the line where the sky and Earth meet.

hydrogen. a colorless gas, the lightest, simplest, and most plentiful substance in the universe.

interplanetary. between planets; in outer space.

kps. kilometers per second.

latitude. a system of measuring, in degrees, the distance north and south of the equator using imaginary lines that run east–west around the Earth.

light-year. the distance a beam of light travels in one year, about 6 trillion miles, used to measure the huge distances to stars, nebulas, and galaxies.

magnitude. a term used to describe a star's brightness.

meteor. the flash of light that a chunk of stone or metal creates when it enters Earth's atmosphere from outer space.

Milky Way. the galaxy that contains our solar system.

moon. a natural satellite of any planet. The Moon is Earth's natural satellite.

mps. miles per second.

myth. traditional story usually about the deeds of gods or heroes.

nebula. a huge cloud of gas and dust among the stars.

North Star. the star Polaris, at the end of the Little Dipper's handle.

orbit. to go around something in a circular pathway.

phases of the Moon. the Moon's changing shapes throughout the month.

planet. a large, spherical body that orbits a star.

the pointers. two stars at the end of the bowl of Big Dipper that aim at the star Polaris.

satellite. a natural celestial body or human-made object that orbits a larger body, usually a planet.

sky sphere. celestial objects appear to be stuck to an imaginary, invisible sphere surrounding Earth.

solar system. the Sun and the planets, moons, asteroids, and comets held captive by its gravity.

speed of light. about 186,000 miles per second.

star. a celestial body; a huge ball of burning gases that creates its own heat and light.

star cluster. a group of stars much smaller than a galaxy, held together by gravity.

Sun. the star at the center of our solar system.

turbulence. an uneven to-and-fro movement of air (or fluid).

zodiac. the belt of sky through which the Sun, Moon, and planets drift. Also, the 12 constellations that lie in this belt.

✦ STAR WORDS

Once you have learned to find the constellations introduced in this book, you will be ready to graduate to a more advanced book on star watching that will include many other constellations.

Three very fine guides are *Exploring the Night Sky* (for young readers), *NightWatch*, and *Summer Stargazing,* all by Terence Dickinson. You will find valuable information on all aspects of astronomy in the monthly magazine *Astronomy* (for all telescope enthusiasts) and the bimonthly *SkyNews* (a Canadian stargazing magazine ideal for beginners).

You'll find that some other books and charts show slightly different ways of connecting the lines of some constellations. There is no hard rule governing the way we illustrate sky figures. In addition, some charts are more detailed than others, and therefore include more stars.

INDEXES

Numbers in brackets refer to
Night Sky Observer's Handbook.

A – Z